# The Whole

# TRUTH

A Poem by

## JAMES CUMMINS

*North Point Press † San Francisco † 1986*

To Maureen Bloomfield

Grateful acknowledgment is made to the following
magazines in which some of the sestinas first appeared:
Antioch Review, Clifton, Iowa Review, Mid-American
Review, Partisan Review, Shenandoah, Sonora Review,
Zone.

I am grateful for the support of the Ohio Arts Council,
in the form of two Individual Artist grants.

I am grateful, too, for the generosity of my friends, in
particular, Elizabeth Armstrong, Ross Feld, James
Hathaway, Jonathan Kamholtz, and David Schloss.

*We wear the mask that grins and lies*

PAUL LAURENCE DUNBAR

# I

# ——— 1

The case seemed cut and dried. Big Ed Fustner, the meat
King, had been caught in an after-hours dive masturbating
Ann Lowenfeld, a socially prominent bowling ball heiress,
With his 'trademark'—a rubber wiener—when a swizzle
Stick turned up in the back of Maurice X., the one-armed
Bathroom attendant who owed Fustner some gambling money.

Mason didn't like Fustner, but there was a lot of money
To be made here. He had to keep Della and Paul in meat
And potatoes. The few grand would be a shot in the arm—
Even if the defense did seem as complex as masturbating.
Mason didn't care if Fustner went to the joint to sizzle
And fry, but then it was Mason the creditors would harass.

Ann Lowenfeld took the stand. She crossed her hairless
Legs, smoothed her bowling shirt. She reeked of money.
Mason fished. "Isn't it true that Fustner just whistles,
And you trot to his table—hotly, spreading your meat?
Didn't it turn you on—the possibility of masturbating
In a public place? Showing it off, defying the long arm

Of the Law?" "So big deal. So he didn't twist my arm!"
She pouted. But Burger was up, his face purple, airless.
"Obviously," he ranted, "Mr. Mason is a master at baiting
A witness! But, Your Honor, it's apparent, for my money,
That for once Mr. Mason's *hectoring* won't get to the meat
Of the issue: the defendant, enraged at Maurice's weasel-

Like attitude, grabbed the nearest weapon, this swizzle—
Uh, 'Exhibit A'—uh, where did I?—uh, by your arm—"
Mason scowled, ignoring him. "Where did you first meet
Ed Fustner?" She flinched. "Are you really an 'heiress'?"
He sneered. "Didn't the dream of Big Ed Fustner's money
Turn you on to another, a lifelong, kind of masturbating?

Furthermore, under that table, just who was masturbating
Whom? Hadn't poor Maurice begged you earlier to 'swizzle
His stick' for him whenever he could get up enough money?
Didn't *you* stab him when he tried to reveal his lost arm
Was now battery-powered—a plaything for an 'heiress'—
For her cold, lonely future, as her body sagged like meat?"

                    †         †         †

"*Masturbating!*" Della gagged. Paul cracked, "*I sing of arm
And a man!*" "Or *heiress*," Burger joked, stabbing a swizzle
Stick in his meat. Mason needled him, "But for *my* money . . ."

# ——— 2

His view blocked by Paul Drake's broad shoulders,
The man on the barstool tried to hold back a sob.
He felt like a stallion trapped in a blind canyon—
The other sheer cliff jailing him was Perry Mason.
"What is this, Mt. Rushmore?"—trying to be funny.
But he saw the game was up, and went along quietly.

The wipers knocked away rain as he confessed quietly.
"I couldn't take it if she gave me the cold shoulder.
Something just . . . *snapped*. Her neck looked so funny.
After I'd killed her—" He hesitated, began to sob.
As usual, for his cue Drake looked over toward Mason,
Then told him about the blonde's house in the canyon,

The wide panes of glass looking over the canyon,
Like those innocent eyes that gaze on life quietly . . .
Drake flipped over a page in his notebook, but Mason
Had had it with this guy blubbering on his shoulder.
The thought really burned him. What kind of S.O.B.
Strangles a girl with her own nylons? He felt funny,

Like the time, as a boy, reading the Sunday funnies,
He saw an episode of exotic torture in Steve Canyon—
A woman garrotted, the balloon over the killer: SOB!
He'd heard his blood then, a creek flowing quietly,
Throwing in relief the dim thunder in his shoulders,
As he twisted the comic like a neck . . . "—Mason . . ."

The lunchmeat had collected himself. "Look, Mason,
I know this scrape I got myself in ain't so funny—
Help me." The car lights swept the road's shoulder.
Mason wanted to force him out, down into the canyon,
Break his neck like a bird's, fiercely and quietly,
Bury him with the memory of the sound of that sob—

That weakness a man admits to in one, strangled sob,
Towering over the beauty he has killed. "*Mr.* Mason,
To you—!" Perry hissed, moving his hands quietly
To that neck. . . The look on Drake's face was funny,
As he fought the car from careening into the canyon,
Adrenalin pumping through his forearms, shoulders. . .

†        †        †

Paul Drake flexed his shoulders. "Boy, it's funny,"
He said quietly. "Tonight, on the rim of the canyon—"
But Mason had rolled up the window of his yellow Saab.

6

# 3

Hamilton Burger cleared his throat. "You see, style
Is just the greater, or lesser, handling of Chance—
The stopping, or delaying, of Time. It's the ability
To manipulate objects by presenting them in a new light.
Say I stand across the courtroom. As I tell the story
Of the crime, the properties of Exhibit A will alter. . ."

Droning on, he seemed to Della a high priest at his altar,
Deciphering an unknown religion's precepts from a stele
Carved in ancient times, and revealing a sacred story
In its lucid figures. "Della," he asked, "what *is* Chance,
Anyway? The representation of the inconstant light—
From which order occurs? The unknowable center? The ability

To posit that which cannot be explained? The probability
All government is but man's need to 'worship,' to alter
His perceptions, to forget. . . ?" Della felt spears of light
Mangle her brain like the shredder in the office. A steel
Ball swung slowly back and forth, leaving nothing to chance:
A real headache. Gazing out her window on the third storey,

She watched a man on the observation deck above. A story
Took hold of her. She saw a man—wife gone, no ability
To pay his debts—cross himself once, then jump. No chance
He'd survive the fall: a twisted bag of garbage on the altar
Of the city, wedding ring, dog tags, wristwatch in the style
Of jewels Mayan virgins wore, diving deep ponds for the Light. . .

Della blinked. The man turned, rose, blotting out the light,
Leaped. She froze, as before her eyes flashed *his* story—
As if *she* were dying, flesh falling through iron and steel:
Bodies banging bone on bone like shutters, the culpability
Of two in marriage—cowards, worshipping an empty altar,
Sacrificing the present to the future, calling it chance . . .

When Della came to, Burger was sucking her toes. "A chance
Encounter?" she murmured. He leaped, red-faced, to the light
Switch. "Fall in me from a great height," she moaned. "Alter
Me . . ." He heard the clank of his zipper. "Tell me a story,
Daddy, the one about the old king's sceptre, its dependability
Unquestioned, rising in the darkest room like shining steel . . ."

†　　　†　　　†

Della exhaled smoke. "Light reading, *that* story. Any chance
Of another?" Burger cursed his disability. "If—if I alter
My approach—" It was no longer just an exercise in style.

# 4

"Perry—" Furious, Mason looked up from the chess
Game he played with himself every night. His mother
Loomed in the doorway, leaning grimly on her walker.
"Perry, turn the heat up? Please? Your father—"
"—Is dead!" Perry raged, his bitter voice rammed
Into the old crone's face. "If you were ambulatory—"

Mason bit it off. He was lucky she was ambulatory
At all, considering the wheezes and grunts her chest
Made, fixing her milk, or peeing: sounds that rammed
Into his skull with all the force of a mother's—!
*Forget it!* But did she have to bring up his father,
How he'd go prowling at night for a streetwalker—

*Somebody who can work her legs without a walker!*—
How little Perry would watch another barely ambulatory
Schizophrenic climb the stairway, while his father
Made growling noises at her shoes, or rubbed her chest.
He couldn't distinguish: father, stairs, whore, mother. . .
Next day at the shopping mall, pushing her up one ramp,

Then alongside the windows, and down another ramp,
Mason thought of the Hitchcock film with Robert Walker:
The pact made to exchange murders. . . Until his mother
Interrupted his thoughts. "I remember being ambulatory.
Before your father—" But her throat caught, her chest
Heaving around that old heart, broken by his father. . .

Like a stake, she drove home her hatred of his father.
"He'd bruise me where it didn't show—*watch that ramp!*—
And ran around with a stripper named 'Community Chest'—
They'd get so tanked up on that damned Johnny Walker—
Until they were both slobbering, just barely ambulatory—!"
She broke down, sobbing. "Perry, I'm not your mother. . .

Hasn't it dawned on you I'm too old to be your mother?
Think back, my baby, try: don't you remember your father
Looming over a woman, her neck broken? The ambulance story,
That she fell—" The wheelchair slipped away down a ramp.
Dazed, Mason watched his grandmother shriek, other walkers
Scatter, as that cage hit a truck. He grabbed his chest. . .

                    †          †          †

Ampules, laboratory, tubes forming a ramp from his chest
To some dials: Mason saw himself hunched over a walker
In a courtroom, pleading his case to his mother and father.

# —— 5

Paul Drake never told Mason he was from Cincinnati.
If it came up, he'd mumble, vaguely, about the 'east.'
Now, as he stood under a streetlight glowing blue
In the night, watching the undersides of the leaves
As they tossed, silver, in the darkness, he felt
The man he was after on this case was himself. . .

The jolt was so strong he dropped ashes on himself.
He brushed frantically at the flame. "Cincinnati—!"
He swore violently, regarding the hole in his felt
Elbow patch. The signpost glowed like a tooth: 'E.
McMillan'—he needed 'W.' As he flipped the leaves
Of his notebook, dreaming, they blended like the blue

Notes of a saxophone, phrasing a passage that blew
Down the lonely streets of his past. He punched himself
In the face: his brain cells were falling like leaves
Under the spell of that old siren, Cincinnati. . .
He thought of Mason's banter, before he'd come east:
"Don't bring me a painting of a bull on black felt!"—

Until, seeing Paul's face, he had asked how he felt.
"With my hands!" But the grin was gone, into the blue,
Rising in the west as the sun rises in the east,
Heading straight for a mid-air collision with himself
In the musical smog of the mind over Cincinnati. . .
As he flew, the years fell away from him like leaves.

Paul crushed his cigarette. Soon, the bus would leave,
Carrying him ever closer to that mirror image he felt
Would at last solve the mystery, the song, of Cincinnati.
Would he grab that wrist, and shout, "Okay, you blew
It, the gorilla suit fooled no one!"—goading himself
To fury at the union, forty years ago, here in the 'east,'

When someone had used the costume of a 'h-hairy b-b-east'
And the words 'M-my little P-Penguin' to seduce, then leave
A mongoloid nun, her womb filling with Paul himself. . .
Finally, the hotel, the toothless night clerk—Paul felt
Clammy, nauseous, as the old man fluttered his pale blue
Eyes: "D-Drake? M-my name, too. Welcome to C-Cincinnati."

† † †

*In his ape mask, Paul felt the blue barrel kick, cleave*
*The clerk's face from east to west* . . . He shook himself—
The clerk was snoring. . . It was evening in Cincinnati.

# —— 6

A big, slow fly, shuffling around the white linen sheets,
Told Perry it was not death he'd bargained for this time—
His world reduced to a vase of freshly painted flowers,
The chrome, tubular sculpture of an engine-operated bed,
A window's gold mosaic, the starched white bust of a nurse,
And the only human voice: the whisper of a shambling fly.

For the first time in weeks, he spoke. "How de time do fly
When yo' havin' fun!" His face turned white as a sheet.
He began again. "Whea de bozz-man—" Panic. "Nurs'!
Nurs'!" He pushed the button once, twice, a third time.
Holy shit! he thought, no longer daring to speak, his bed
Soaked with sweat. Pulling the card from the red flowers,

Unthinking, he read aloud. "Jes' hopin' dese flowers. . ."
Now Perry screamed. "Wuz *happenin'*?" Slowly, the fly
Wheeled around the room again, plopped wearily on the bed.
"Yo' a nigger now," it buzzed. Perry snorted. "Shee-*yit!*"
He denied. Then screamed again. "Man, yo' doin' hard time,
Mostly jes' fo' bein' white. Hey, no use callin' de nurs'—

Yo' on de cardiac flo', an' everboddy kno' ain't no nurs'
Runnin' to no nigger!" The fly hummed "Hearts & Flowers,"
As Perry tried to remember the past, the length of time
Since his heart attack. Blindly, he hated, blamed, the fly—
Too much himself, a speck against the white hill of sheets,
Alone. The fly chuckled, "Don' pollyticks make strange bed-

Fellahs?" wagging its head. "Dis wurl' yo' makes yo' *own* bed—"
A stricken Perry was in earnest discourse with a fly. The nurse
Came with his bedpan, to jack up the bed and change the sheets.
Silent, sly, neither one breathed as she arranged the flowers—
Only their eyes, a thousand and two of them, moved. "Damn fly!"
She roared, rolling a magazine. "I'll get that fly this time!"

Perry heaved his huge body into hers, caught her arm in time,
Sent both of them crashing through the TV stand onto the bed.
She bit, shrieked, as he shouted, "Git yo' ass in *gear,* fly!
*Move!*" and six orderlies came running to the aid of the nurse,
Subduing him finally by beating him with the vase of flowers,
Snowing him under an avalanche of white coats and sheets . . .

† † †

Flowers, window, bed . . . The nurse shrugged, "I saw a fly—"
Then male voices: " . . . Huge . . . Need straps . . . Last time . . ."
But to Mason, they had come: fierce horsemen in white sheets . . .

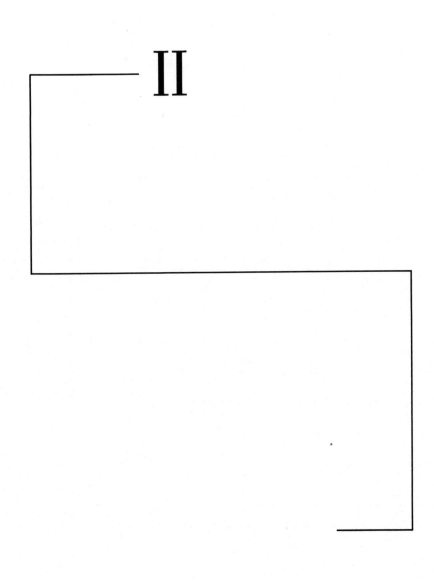

II

# ——— 7

Perry and the fly were debating the question of animality.
"We choose a totem as the image of the cry we make inside
One night, our mouths no longer able to surround, contain,
The fiery death of the brain in the face of too much . . ."
"Yeah? So how come yo' talk lak me when yo' open yo' mouf'?"
"Foucault," Perry fudged, "would say, *As death is the limit*

*Of human life in the realm of time, madness is its limit—*
Perry paused theatrically—*in the realm of animality . . .*"
"Say *whut?*" But Perry stuffed a thermometer in his mouth
Hurriedly, as a nurse entered. "It's too nice to be inside,
Isn't it?" she said cheerfully. Perry felt she had too much
Lipstick on. Glaring, he indicated that his mouth contained

A thermometer. "Not *that* thermometer! Those jars contain
Rectal—!" She guffawed as Perry spat. *That's the limit!*
He blew up. He went for her. *A man can only take so much!*
The fly shrieked, "Sho'ly we enterin' de realm ob' *animality!*"
As it hopped up and down on Perry's shoulder. "Git inside
Her *pants*, man! Go fo' it! Stuff yo' tube into dat *mouf*!"

But Perry had other ideas about her mascara, her red mouth.
Launching his whale-like body toward her, his mind contained
Alien, yet familiar pictures, welling up from deep inside—
They roared on savagely, an unbroken stream, without limit,
Arcing through the dim past: a fudgesickle, Ann O'Malley's T-
Shirt, wettened by a hose, Aunt Ginny's nylon hose, too much

Of her legs, his mother's legs, at an odd angle . . . "Too much,"
Winked the doctor, stuffing a pill into Perry's slack mouth.
He wagged his head. "The awesome force of the anima . . . Lithi-
Um is what he needs, the only thing that'll help him contain
Life and sanity in what, let's face it, is a seemingly limit-
Less expanse of flesh." Turning, he touched the nurse inside

Her blouse, lips squirming all over her face. "Oh, yes, inside
Me . . ." she moaned. The fly blinked all its eyes. "Too much,
Man, dey's too much! Jes' looka dat. If dey ain't de limit!"
Catatonic, his face stony as an oracle's cave, Perry's mouth
Opened: *"The configuration of animal spirits the body contains
Activates to save itself . . . thus succumbing to animality . . ."*

&#8224;  &#8224;  &#8224;

"Too much whut's inside yo' *brain* sh'd be inside her *mouf*!"
Under a cold, clear moon, the fly watched his friend contain,
In his hand's rhythmic motion, the limits of his animality . . .

# —— 8

Burger put down his coat, hat, and a bottle of red wine
As he smirked, "Guess who attacked another nurse today?"
"No!" Della muffled a giggle. "What'd she do this time—
Step on a cockroach?" They roared. Hamilton had tears
In his eyes. "Maybe he thought she was a *Spanish* fly!"
Nearly choking, Della got the phone. "It's your mother."

She deepened her voice. *"Hey, muthuh! It's yo' muthuh!"*
Burger collapsed on the table, knocking over the wine—
A twitching bag of flesh, like a rabbit hit on the fly.
"Hello? *No!*" Covering the phone, he said, "On AS TODAY,
TOMORROW, the new soap, a lawyer in a psych ward tears
Skin off his knees to be a young kid again!" "What time?"

Della asked. *"Toon in tomorruh, same chan'l, same time—"*
"Shh-h-h!" Burger said. Then: "Yes, Mother. Yes, Mother.
Yes, Mother!" *"Yo' Honnuh, suh!"* Della saluted, tears
Streaming down her face. "No, we haven't opened the wine
Yet, Mother. Just an inside joke, is all. See, today
He jumped a nurse . . ." *"Wuz jes' tryin' t' open his fly!"*

Della yelled over his shoulder. "Huh? No, Mother, a *fly!*
Della wanted me to swat a fly! Listen, it's about time
For dinner, so be seeing you. And don't call anymore today,
Okay? You know I *always* pull it back and wash there, Mother!
I will. Good-bye." Two things made Burger flush: red wine
And his mother. As he stared over his glass at Della's tear-

Stained face, he saw only his mother's, bursting into tears.
Della sobbed, "My face is a leg-hold trap. Perry and a fly
Talk all day long, and what do *I* do? Cry and drink wine!"
Burger sneered, "Della and her torch. Remember the time
He made you jack him off in the D. A.'s office?" "Mother-
Fucker! You pompous motherfucker!" she screamed. "The day

You could carry his briefcase—!" "Della, honey, today
Your face *looks* like his briefcase!" He watched her tears,
Her eyes spurting hydrants of regret, replace his mother's
Power to inspire guilt and revulsion. She *looked* like a fly,
A bug he wanted to squash, a ball against which he'd time
The swing of a bat. Aroused, Burger slugged down his wine.

&#8224;  &#8224;  &#8224;

"I hate you!" Della whined. "No! Not this time, not today—"
But Burger pushed her face down to his fly. "Use those tears
As a lubricant!" he hissed. "We'll see who's the *bad muthuh*!"

# —— 9

A silent Perry remembered how it used to be: look
Hard at all the faces, figure out who's a killer.
Consider the money, that was always the best clue—
The only way you got the older ones into the game.
But, of course, money was never the real question.
The real question was, does it all end in silence?

He'd been very good at cracking someone's silence—
Watching the eyes, the critical moment when a look
Betrayed the fear he would ask the fatal question.
And he *would* ask. Without mercy. He was a killer.
He loved the chance to destroy, like flushing game
From the field of a face, each tiny twitch a clue,

Small animals of fear he tracked down, clue by clue,
Stuffing them, one by one, into the jury's silence.
It took brutality to get to this level of the game.
You had to be a hall of mirrors, give back the look
Of infinite self-loathing that spurs on the killer.
You had to be his conscience, with its one question

Pounding his brain like beaters, until that question
Drove him screaming out into the clearing of a clue,
Blinking frantically in the sun, to face his killer,
As around him the bleak farmland became the silence
Of the courtroom, his face lit up with the wild look
Of one who has outlived his usefulness in the game . . .

Perry whispered through the bars of the door, "Game?"
Outside, an intern looked up from his pad, a question
In his eyes. A nurse, marking a chart, saw his look.
"Used to be a lawyer. He's wanting his game of CLUE
In a bit. He plays a while, then lapses into silence.
He's probably hot on the trail of some crazy killer—

You know, up here." She tapped her head. "A killer?"
She nodded, twirling a finger around her ear. "Game?"
Perry heard himself say. *Does it all end in silence?*
"Game?" he repeated slyly, posing that meek question
As if trying to trick some green rookie from the ACLU.
The intern hid behind his magazine. He wouldn't look.

†     †     †

Questions. Shrewd looks. A fiercely guarded silence.
When it came to playing CLUE, the old bag was a killer.
"Game?" Warily, Perry tossed the dice. "Game? Game?"

## ──── 10

"I'll tell you one thing: I'd sure like to suck *her*
Tits!" Tragg swung his beefy fist over to his drink.
Paul watched his shrunken shoulders swaying in time
To the music, his medallion bouncing as his big head
Wobbled around in its collar. "*Arthur!*" His wife,
Red, winked conspiratorially at Paul. "Such an act!"

"Yeah?" Tragg slurred. "If it's such a goddamn act,
*You* oughta get caught in the middle of it! Suck *her*
Tits," Tragg winked at Paul, nodding toward his wife,
"Your lips'll pucker for a week!" He took his drink
And rolled the icy, sweating glass over his forehead.
Furious, the woman hissed, "It's this way every time,

Isn't it? You wait and wait, then pick the best time
To make me out a fool!" Tragg backed down. "Aw, act
Your age," he whined. Red took aim at that huge head,
Revolving like a moose in a penny arcade. "Suck *her*
Tits? How about mine for a change?" "Uh, your drink,"
Paul interjected. "Like another?" "This is my wife,"

Tragg snorted bitterly. "My lovely, beautiful wife . . .
You see she knows as much about having a good time—"
"Tragg, I—" "*Good time?*" Red knocked over a drink.
"Maybe my idea of a *good time* is performing a sex act
You can't even remember: ol' In-And-Out! *Go* suck her—
Isn't that your philosophy? The only way to get ahead

Is to give it?" Paul felt the drums roll in his head.
He sopped the drink with a napkin, smiled at the wife.
"Hey, you two, easy! Let's—" "You wanna suck her,
Too?" Red sneered. "So come up and see *me* some time!"
Paul felt her foot slide up his pants leg. "Be an act
Of mercy," Tragg grumbled. Paul gulped down his drink.

The dancer's flesh was a fountain singing, *Drink, Drink,*
As she swung her breasts in a slow arc over Paul's head.
Lights dimmed, the band got hot: he was part of the act,
Her movement caressing, immersing him. Tragg, his wife—
Vanished in the hypnotic twirl of her breasts, in time
With the drum roll, a mandala conjuring, giving succor . . .

†        †        †

"Did you see those suckers?" Tragg bellowed at his wife.
"What an act! What an *act*!" Paul held his aching head.
"Come on, Drake, drink up! We're having a swell time!"

"I *may* have made a mistake. Whew! This stuff is heavy!"
Perry held the silver roach-holder with its glowing roach
Over to the fly, who puffed with obvious pleasure. "Man,"
His little friend exhaled, "this stuff'll comb yo' face!"
Footsteps hurrying by the door to the shock therapy room
Startled them. "Shhh-hh!" Perry motioned with his hand.

The corridor was silent. After a minute, he let his hand
Drop, as flesh drops after an electric jolt. "Too heavy,
Man," he giggled, "too *heavy*!" The fly hooted. The room
Echoed with their muffled laughter. "Hey, gimme de roach,
Man." As he held the roach, Perry studied the fly's face.
Middle-aged, soon to be old, it was the face of an old man

Still young. He never knew what it would say next. "Man,"
It exhaled with satisfaction, "why yo' take whut dey hand
Out?" Perry bucked, as if he'd been punched in the face.
He took a big hit. Smoke felt thick on his tongue, heavy.
"Keep it up," he joked, "I'll ditch you for the cute roach
Up there on that strap!" The fly snorted. "She need room

To breathe, man. Too fast fo' yo'. An' yo' ain't no *room*,
Man, yo' de entire *buildin'*, if yo' git mah meanin', man."
Perry got the meaning. He cracked up. "Back off, roach!"
The fly hopped from Perry's shoulder to his arm to his hand.
"Back off, waterbug! Dis is *mah* suckah. He ain't heaby—
He mah *bro'*!" The fly guffawed. Perry could feel his face

Stretch, bend, twist, until it no longer resembled a face,
He was laughing so hard. The fly circled the enormous room
Once, sat down. It chuckled. "Ah'll say dis shit is heaby.
Got me talkin' to *roaches*! An' dose muthafuckahs, mah man,
Don' kno' *shit*!" The fly grinned as Perry offered his hand.
It took a big hit. "Let's gib de roach a hit ob de roach!"

Perry shook his head. "Jail bait." He sucked on the roach;
The fly blew out smoke. "Ah kno'," it sighed, making a face.
It propped its head up on its wings, relaxed in Perry's hand.
"Pat Boone," Perry said suddenly. "I'd sit alone in my room,
Grooving on Pat Boone." The fly was zonked out. "Oh, man,
Yo' run some heaby riffs," it giggled. "Yo' riffs is *heaby*!"

                    †          †          †

"Christ! Even his arm is heavy!" The nurse flicked a roach
Off Perry's hand, then strapped it down. He watched the face
Of the man who swabbed his temples. A hush filled the room.

# —— 12

*Everybody knows!* That was his first thought,
As he stumbled, at lunch, from the courtroom.
He couldn't shake off the grip of his desire:
To get down on his knees, slip off her shoe,
Slowly run his hand along her stockinged foot,
Then lift it to his lips, and kiss her toes...

Thoughts like these kept Hamilton on his toes.
Already some of them were watching, he thought,
To see if his eyes travelled from foot to foot,
Staring at the stockinged legs around the room,
Until one let a heel slip gently from its shoe,
Revealing to him the naked object of his desire.

But worse than fear of public shame, the desire
To lick and suck Miss Weston's beautiful toes—
Pink and beige, poking out of her upraised shoe—
Ignited him, as at the stake, his every thought
A stick of kindling, the air circling him a room
Of flame, flickering like an undulating foot...

Out in the hallway, shifting from foot to foot,
He bound himself over to the rituals of desire.
Eyes glazed, he drifted back in time to the room
Where a child knelt before his mother, her toes
Sensual, erect, as he stroked them. He thought
Of how that child removed, so tenderly, her shoe.

The judge blew open the restroom door. "Ah-*choo!*"
She sneezed by, toilet paper sticking to her foot,
A hearing aid banging on her head like a thought,
A voice, appealing the stiff sentence of desire . . .
At the salad bar, the chickpeas gleamed like toes.
Hamilton smoked, stared over the court lunchroom,

As memory and need led him down room after room,
Whispers and flames licking the sole of each shoe,
Until finally he could see, up ahead, the cold toes
Of the goddess, her beckoning, monumental foot. . .
His face flickered like a votive candle as desire
Danced, a barefoot goddess, through his thought. . .

        †       †       †

Night slipped its foot into its black pump shoe.
The stars gleamed like toes over the cold bedroom,
Flickers of desire. *Or chickpeas*, Hamilton thought.

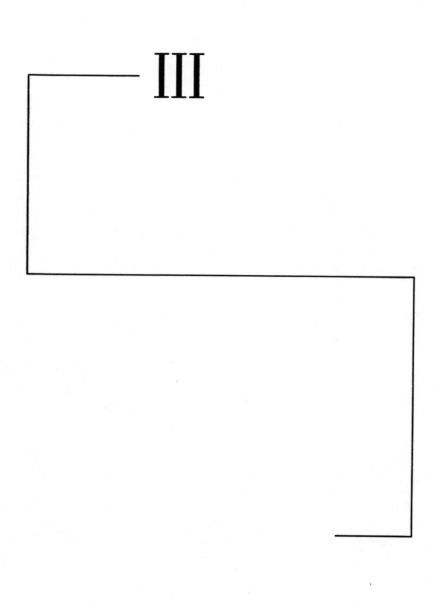

# III

# ——— 13

*There is the danger Foucault is conflating, under the term 'madness,'*
*Two entirely different concepts: the historical designation by a power*
*Which dominates what is other to it—what is barbarous and menacing—*
*By repressing it, enclosing it in particular coded figures; and the deep-*
*Rooted, transhistorical instance which is present at base in any social*
*Bond, and which we may as well call—Perry shuddered—'the Forbidden.'*

Perry and the fly shifted their weight on the toilet seat. "*Forbidden . . .*"
Perry brooded. "That's the one that gets me." The fly chuckled. "*Madness*
Ain't so hot, neither," it said. "Roun' here, it be de Numero Uno social
Disease!" Perry nodded. "Almost makes you believe in some higher Power—
You know?" The fly groaned. "Uh-oh. Wheah mah boots? It's gettin' *deep*
In heah. Hey, man, if whut yo' *is* is considered 'barbarous an' menacin,'

An' yo' is boxed away, yo' boxes away whutever is 'barbarous an' menacin'
Inside yo', too. Because yo' think dey is *right!* Only thing 'forbidden'
Is thinkin' dey might be *wrong!*" His chin in his palm, in a revery deep
As dream, Perry murmured assent, as a sleeper nods assent to dream madness.
"White boy, jes' starin' into nuthin' but hisself—don' yo' kno' power
Got to be a *personal* thing? Yo' gotta slap de flesh, boy: dat's de social

Bond yo' lift *yo'* hand in homage to. Win or lose, when yo' slap de social
Flesh, yo' sayin' to de Man yo' *kno'* it all a game. *Barbarous an' menacin'*
Yo' ain't: yo' can't go runnin', tryin' to look lak de mirror ob *his* power!
Yo' got to look wid' lobe on other *people*, man: dat's whut is 'forbidden'!
De Man keep us apart, he keep us mad. An' anythin' but lobe's jes' madness."
Slowly, Perry lifted one eyelid. He whispered, "It begins as a sound, deep

In the ear, the sound the sea makes in a shell. It's *memory*, sounding deep
In the mind, a distant fire advancing—until the ethical man, the social
Man, is overtaken, engulfed, a fireball running, screaming in his madness—"
"An' his three-piece suit!" the fly needled. "He's *barbarous and menacing*
Enough *now!*" Perry retorted. "And it's this manifestation of the *Forbidden*—
The unnatural become natural—that shakes the movers-and-shakers in power:

Because it is a mirror!" Perry grunted, sighed. A turd splashed. "Power,"
He went on, as the fly grabbed its nose, "is the obverse of fear, the deep-
Rooted pact man makes with humiliation." The fly said, "So whut's *forbidden*
Is all equal: usin' de wrong fork an' fuckin' yo' sister in de ass?" "Social
Games," Perry sneered, "social games. The one, true 'barbarous and menacing'
Humiliation is, simply, Death. The rest is merely hall-of-mirrors madness. . ."

†     †     †

"Barbie-Doll-Dennis-the-Menacing!" was how Perry pooh-poohed 'the *Forbidden*.'
A deep sarcasm scoring his words, he made fun of the fly's sense of a social
Order. "In dis wurl'," Perry snickered, "power is sanity. Love is madness."

# ——— 14

Paul Drake liked the cut of his jib. He listened to this man
Named Mo Fugger, who dropped some Alka-Seltzer into his water,
Watched the bubbles flower, climb the glass for long seconds,
Then spoke. "English. That is, you know, until I found a bag
Man don't need a college degree." His voice was bitter, hard.
"I was tough. A boxer. But they made me hang up the gloves.

Bought me ten grey suits. Oh, they handled me with kid gloves,
At first. Expense account, leased a Benz for me. Then the man
Sent me on short trips, out of the country. I had to be hard—
Had to kick some ass, you know?" He gulped the medicinal water.
"They were testing me. Whether I was ready for a 'body bag,'
They said. Corporate humor. But then I met my first 'second'—

You know, the contact. The guy I deliver to. In a few seconds,
I knew it was all over. Just like a hand sliding into a glove:
Different parts of me falling down separate alleys, fuckin' bags
You land at the bottom of and wait, alone . . . So I wasn't a man
Anymore. You know?" Paul ordered himself a scotch-and-water.
He was silent for a while, then he asked, "So it was real hard?"

Fugger gazed blearily. "Whaaa? Was what what? Really hard—?"
He laughed, embarrassed. "Oh, you mean . . . God, for a second—!"
He slumped down. "Never mind." He drank the last of the water,
Then sipped his Bloody Mary. "When I'm on a job, I wear gloves."
He paused. "Get it? You gumshoes are always looking for a *man*—
What about *machines*? I'm a well-paid *machine*! See these bags

Under my eyes?" Paul saw the spittle on his lips. "Moneybags!"
Fugger laughed loudly. "Moneybags! Think if I gotta pull hard
Time one attache case holds the dough? You gotta be kidding, man.
Know what's in these bags? Knowledge. Knowledge of the seconds
I got left. . . I'm a fuckin' hawk on somebody's arm. With a glove
On my head. He takes it off, and I fly away . . . over the water . . .

But if I look as if I understand, if I'm a threat—" "What're
You ol' boys drinkin'?" a new voice boomed. "Hey, fuckface, bag
It!" roared another. Mo knocked the Bloody Mary over his gloves,
As a burly man in a CAT cap punched him in the arm. "Whoa, hard
Guy!" Mo smiled, shamefaced. His head wobbled. "Wait a second!
Not that spy shit again? What you tellin' this nice young man?"

†     †     †

Paul fiddled with his scotch-and-water. Mo wiped off his gloves.
An old man hobbled into the bar. He carried a grimy shopping bag.
For seconds, Paul thought about his father. He was breathing hard.

# ——— 15

Perry and the fly walked into the dingy conference room.
Seated around the circular table, in front of large cups
Of coffee and small tin ashtrays, fourteen haggard faces
Glanced up as one at the hulking, beetle-browed presence
In a blue hospital gown, Hush Puppies, and MR. PEANUT tie.
A short, portly man with long hair and a beard—a poet

From the college who had received a grant to teach poet-
Ry to the mentally disturbed—indicated there was room
Near him. Perry sat down, fingering his MR. PEANUT tie
Nervously. The fly drifted lazily over the coffee cups.
"Presence," the man was saying. "You establish presence
In a poem by the authenticity of experience." The faces

Nodded slowly. Some dozed off. Perry watched the faces
Carefully, sensing one of them would hate him. The poet
Continued. "Often, a young poet shows great prescience,
Even about his own future . . . But look around this room:
How many of you thought you'd end up here?" Three cups
Spilled, twenty hands lit cigarettes. "A MR. PEANUT tie

Can't save you from experience. Right, MR. PEANUT Tie?"
Perry felt his stomach drop. Grimly, the lunatic faces
Swung toward him. The fly swooped down. "All dem cups
Runnin' ovah, man. Let's split." But the college poet
Was being honest. "For instance, say a poem is a room.
Say you're throwing a party. Just look at your present

State—would you invite yourself to a party? *Presence*
Is not just *personality*. Do you agree, MR. PEANUT Tie?"
Perry trembled, his mouth dry. He saw, across the room,
In drug-like clarity, an old woman shake some dry faeces
From a styrofoam cup. One man had written the word *poet*
On his notebook in pinpricks of blood. A girl's hiccups

Echoed in the silence. Perry sweated. *Hiccup. Hiccup:*
More loudly, more loudly, until it was another presence,
Stalking through the room. His face contorted, the poet
Demanded a response. "MR. PEANUT Tie? MR. PEANUT Tie?"
Perry threw his head back. He frowned on all the faces.
"Yes," he croaked. "Yes!" Then stumbled from the room.

†      †      †

Perry was ecstatic. In the sad room, in their presence,
In the smoke over styrofoam cups, in his MR. PEANUT tie,
He faced the faces, spoke. In his own voice. The poet.

# —— 16

Della glanced up at Hamilton, who was licking her feet.
"Oh," she murmured, adjusting a pillow behind her head.
"Oh, that last one really got to me." Moving her legs,
She rubbed first one foot, then the other over his face.
"Do my toes now," Della commanded him. "Put your mouth
On them, *now*! Oh, god, I love it when you do my toes!"

Della couldn't understand this obsession with her toes.
She wanted him hung up on her breasts, not on her feet.
Often, she caught herself staring at Hamilton's mouth—
Blind as a newborn's, giving her toes, as it were, head.
Della understood the ritual, what it wanted of her face:
Slight sneer, yet aroused in spite of herself, her legs

Eager to fling apart, really more like arms than legs—
The only embrace Della could make him feel. Did toes—
Or the pleasing of them—connect somehow to the face
At the other end? Was it that only by worshipping feet
Could he hope to appease a goddess, whose distant head
Spat fire or balm toward him from her terrifying mouth?

Della thought of Hamilton's mother, covering her mouth
Daintily, to break up the particles of a belch, her legs
Crossed primly and hooked at the ankles. Did that head
Realize what she'd done to her son with her cruel toes?
Della had to giggle. Hamilton looked up from her feet.
She made the giggle a moan, artfully arranging her face

To his lust, lowering her lids to better watch his face:
Not only had he bought it, but his moist, earnest mouth
Had turned her on. Did she imagine it, or did her feet
Seem to tingle, come alive? Impatience moved her legs,
As if his lips had lit a tip of a long fuse in her toes,
That ran along her body toward an explosion in her head.

Della saw half her foot disappear into Hamilton's head.
She pushed it in. It was like fucking him in the face.
No wonder Mama had dug it. Her nipples felt like toes.
Then he was inside her, breathless mouth atop her mouth,
Fire flying along its fuse as she held him with her legs.
"Curl my feet, motherfucker," she moaned, "curl my feet."

†       †       †

Della rubbed Hamilton's legs. She fondled his flat feet.
Then, one by one, she sucked his toes. She made a face.
Mouth open, Hamilton snored. Della stroked his damp head.

# 17

Perry picked up a copy of Robert Lowell's THE DOLPHIN.
He tried to figure out the formative principle, the art.
What were the 'flashing fish'? Did they have big fins?
Do you eat them with 'servile sausages' (had he got that
Right?) after cooking them in a heavy, but tasty, grease?
Or was that long ago? And this another, different life?

"So yo' all call dat livin'?" asked the fly, of that life.
"That's not the point," Perry said patiently. "The dolphin
Symbolizes man's voyage in rough seas, each wave a crease
In a forehead behind which swims a crazed desire for art,
For order. Its up-and-down movement is a reminder that
Sanity is cyclical: the sea is McClean's, you need big fins

To swim through it." "Ah heah yo' needs quite a few fins
To git *in* it!" the fly pouted. "It's a metaphor for life!"
Perry said, annoyed. "Forget about money. He says that
The genealogy, the line, of the image goes from the Dauphin
Of Joan of Arc, to the one Yeats said, in the sea of art,
Is man's best friend." "Did yo' see dat movie, GREASE?

Now, Ah wouldn' mind slidin' mah sausage thro' *dat* grease!
Yo' go talk 'bout *art*, jes' gimme *life*!" "Dat's ob-*fins*-
Ive!" mocked Perry. "Anyway, look: you used a work of art
To look behind the work of art itself, trying to see *life*!
Lowell takes the dolphin image down to the Miami Dolphins
Because he saw in their No-Name Defense the anonymity that

Allows perfection. He felt humiliated by a genealogy that
Coated the art, the form he tried to embrace, the way grease
Coats pigs at a county fair. On the other hand, the dolphin
Is constantly cleansed by waves of anxiety, its big fins
Hand-holds allowing him to ride it, becoming his own art. . .
When he did that, he didn't have to think about his life."

"Ah kin unnerstan' dat! Ah don' wan' think 'bout his life,
Neither!" Perry smiled, amused. How could he explain that
This was the repose resulting from the criticism of art?
Suddenly, beatifically, came a moment to which few grease-
Monkeys of literature gain access: he watched the big fins
Lift up, seeking him, on a wave, heard the crying dolphin:

†       †       †

*Remember that Lowell sought from me the big finis, the art*
*Of the life made whole . . . I gave him his body, its grease.*
*But know he learned, at the last, any cab might be a dolphin.*

"I—I could still lose it." In despair, Perry put his head in his hands.
"Sheee-yit!" Annoyed, the fly clicked its long legs together like bones.
Perry stared gloomily. "All anything anyone ever says is just projection,"
He muttered. "Aw, whuh th' fu' yo' talkin' 'bout, man?" scolded the fly.
It nibbled an Oreo. "Yo' talks to me, don' yo'? Ah talks to yo', right?"
The fly grinned up at him. "All ennyboddy evah gits is jes' language . . ."

Perry's ear lifted up like a receiver, a huge dish of flesh. "Language,"
The fly crooned, "be de greates' tool dat de Lawd evah put in our hands!
Iff'n yo' mind tips too far one way, den de language gonna put it right.
Iff'n someone tells yo' a good story, man, yo' feel it deep in yo' bones.
Wid'outs de language, man, how could yo' an' me—a lawyer an' a fly—
Talk 'bout things? Nex' thing yo' kno', yo' be sayin' *Ah'm* a projection!"

Perry sat up. He regarded the fly with alarm. *Was* it only a projection?
And if it was, what the hell of? "Dey's all diff'ren' kinds ob language,
Man," the fly continued. "Ah mean, how do yo' kno' Ah alluz wuz a fly?
Dey's de language ob trees, de language ob dancin', de language ob hands.
An' wheah Ah learn to talk dis way? Mebbe Ah'm jes' de language ob bones
Dat yo' white face need to heah so's Ah kin put yo' silly language right!

An' mebbe Ah'm nuthin', yo' kno'? Yo' says everboddy's nuthin', right?"
Perry felt the words scald, purify. If the fly were really a projection,
It was of a language hidden away inside, buried deep in his weary bones,
Yet supporting him—his means of searching the world, his cold language
Of reason, logic—in the way his skeleton lifted his head, arms, hands,
In the calculated movements before a judge, so much like prayer. The fly

Waited patiently, watching as Perry considered the language of the fly.
The TV shook like a tambourine. *Put yo' silly language right right right*:
The phrase echoed through Perry's brain. Gently, he raised his big hands,
As if to stay its flight. His hands turned, in air, lifting a projection
Of a silver chalice, filled with blood. Perry couldn't speak. "Language
Is holy, man," said the fly. "Not jes' cuz it's *holy*, not cuz yo' bones

Cry out to listen. It's holy cuz it's greatah dan enny bag ob shit bones
Lak yo' kin evah kno'! Yo' don' *kno'* de things yo' don' kno'!" The fly
Spat. "Yo' think de word *fuck* be 'de way one heahs de primitibe language
Ob feelin'!' Oh, *man*! Language kno' dat it can't be whut it ain't, right?
So it alluz laughin' at itself, man! An' yo' don' kno' dat! Projection?
Man, yo' lak Pilate. Only thing in life be clean enuf is yo' own hands!"

† † †

"Birt' to bones, man," the fly yawned, "all ennyboddy gits is language . . ."
The fly stretched once, closed all its eyes, curled up in Perry's hand.
"Iff'n Ah'm a projection, man, don' yo' worry. Some day we git it right."

42

IV

# —— 19

It seemed from that moment on, Perry calmed down,
Marching to that "different drummer," so to speak.
He quickly secured his release by out-arguing them.
Some of them accepted this defeat as "good therapy,"
While the smarter ones among them at least thought
He had what it took to survive: he was an asshole.

Perry knew it took an asshole to know an asshole—
How else can you tell when the shit is coming down?
I'm no longer as young as I used to be, he thought.
I have to play the game from the other side: speak
In many voices, outwit them at their own "therapy,"
Scare them off with what I can find out about *them*.

Because they'll get you. It's what matters to them.
You don't let them get you, hey, you're an asshole.
Simple as that. Their pious crap about "therapy"—
They just want to kick your balls when you're down.
I had them running in circles when I wouldn't speak.
They would have given plenty to know what I thought.

The poet is the leader of the Quest, Perry thought.
*He is a member of the group, yet he also leads them.*
Perry started, wildly. Had he heard someone speak?
*It's no wonder they think you're a flaming asshole!*
Alarmed, Perry poured himself a drink to calm down.
Silence . . . Drowsily, he mused: I survived therapy.

Group therapy, T.A. therapy, poetry therapy, therapy
Therapy. Start my own brand of therapy, he thought.
Maple therapy. For saps. He felt a little bit down,
As if even thinking about them was giving in to them.
Then, bolting up, Perry heard. *Wake up, you asshole!*
In an odor of raw sewage, the voices began to speak.

*You gab so much, we thought we'd never get to speak.*
*We come to help you with the words. But get a serape,*
*For god's sake. Look oracular. You are an asshole:*
*Make it work for you. Nobody cares what you thought.*
*Or think. And you are way too hung up about "them."*
*You ought to worry about us. We're on our way down.*

†     †     †

Great. Yeats gets roses, I get assholes, he thought.
Therapy was better than this. He heard one of them
Speak. *I'm Diana Ross, beefcheeks. Let's get down.*

## 20

How strong life is, to resist our need to die.
We stuff ourselves with food, knowing that food
Rots, and waits in us, rotting. We make money
Instead of things, an abstraction that creates
Unnatural dependence. Of our vices, only sex
Rewards our fear. It is the only vice we hate.

We trick our loves up, in costumes that we hate,
Carry creased photos in our wallets until we die.
One prepares us for, one helps us finish, sex—
We don't know which is which: which is the food,
Which is the appetite, which is the one creates
Desire, which one desire creates. And the money,

The hatred of the gods made manifest, the money
Drops even as a leopard leaps, its power to hate
The body most awesome of the powers man creates.
The earth gives up its secrets, to help us die:
All manner of things to be combined, as food
Results from calculation, as bodies join in sex.

Diana said, *Bible freak scare your mom? Is sex
All you ever think about? Huh? Sex and money?
It's pretty clear you're not hung up about food.*
"Look, I know you're trying to help, but I hate
This *grilling*. I can't help what I am. The die
Is cast. I'm the image of what our lie creates."

*Whose voice is silent in the image Donne creates?*
He wrote. *Only a man could say that, after sex,*
*We die.* Diana laughed, *Only thing that* he'd *die*
*Of is not getting into her pants! For my money,*
*You just want to fuck the bitches that you hate.*
"I don't want to fuck anyone!" he shouted. *Food*

*Time!* Diana taunted him. *Go kitchen! Get food!*
He rose from his desk. You are what you create,
He grumbled. He *was* a bit hungry. And he'd hate
To miss IRONSIDE. Diana whispered, *A little sex*
*Later? We could pretend I'm doing you for money.*
He heard her giggle. *It's the only way to die . . .*

&#8224;     &#8224;     &#8224;

*Money shoots through us like a drug until we die.*
On FAMILY FEUD, Dawson's grins were full of hate.
*Amateurs "have sex,"* Diana cooed. *A pro creates.*

## 21

*All the best baseball managers play against The Book,*
*Gauging from a mythic wisdom to the current reality.*
*So one always plays against what one does, one's art.*
*In this dialogue is the "line": that arc between here*
*And there, the near face and the far. (And your face,*
Diana teased, *allows for a particularly* long *line . . .)*

Perry paused. He had to laugh. "Okay, a good line,"
He conceded. "Too bad we can't use it in our book."
He gazed out over his typewriter, seeing Diana's face
In the way blind men will stare into another reality.
"You look pretty today," he said softly. "Come here."
Un-unh, Diana answered. *The big boy's doing his Art—*

*Far be it from me to interrupt a big boy and his Art!*
*Anyway, I've asked someone to help you with your line.*
*Gustave? "Gustave Flaubert?" Gus, can you come here?*
"Gustave Flaubert?" Perry repeated, incredulous. Book
Or no book, he had to hear this master of pure reality.
"Gustave Flaubert?" he repeated a third time, his face

Lit up with the light that will light up a child's face.
*Monsieur, that is my name.* To Perry, Flaubert was Art
Deified, a god taking up a brief residence in reality.
"I've read all your books," he said humbly. *The line—*
Flaubert paused. *Merci, that's very nice. Which book*
*Did you like best? Do please speak up. I do not hear*

*So well anymore.* Perry named his favorite. *Ah, here
I am understood! Voilà! Mine, also.* As Perry's face
Glowed, Flaubert said, *I'm told you are writing a book?
Do you understand ignoble man is redeemed only by Art?
That Art must become a religion to you? That the line
Must be to your own thought as God's Word is to reality?*

*Sort of?* Diana's voice brought Perry back to reality:
*We better go back, Gus. You've been very helpful here.*
Perry thought he heard the rustle of notes. *The line—
Gus, really, it's been swell.* Then Perry saw his face:
Briefly illumined, the glorious old man's face *was* Art.
Radiant, tender, Gus shone above the pages of his book.

†　　　†　　　†

*The Game of Art is played*, he wrote, *between the lines
Of Reality.* Perry put down his and Gus's favorite book.
*Here,* he said to himself. *Here.* And covered his face.

# —— 22

*Apart from the pulling and hauling stands what I am,*
*Stands amused, complacent, compassionating, idle, unitary,*
*Looks down, is erect, or bends an arm on an impalpable certain rest,*
*Looking with side-curved head curious what will come next,*
*Both in and out of the game and watching and wondering at it . . .*
*I have no mockings or arguments, I witness and wait . . .*

Perry put down the book, gazed out the window, let the weight
Of the words sink into him . . . "It hits at just what I am,
Too," he mused. The night kicked up sparks. He watched it
Wheel its iron shoes past his head, roar over the Unitari-
An church on the corner, set fire to buildings in the next
Block. "My profession teaches me I'm better than the rest

Of them . . . My life, that I'm low as a convict, and the rest
Of the forgotten. I'm a nothing, in the middle of his wait,
Suffering the terror of confluence: my own body, and next
Year . . ." The fire outside turned his face orange. *I am*
*Nothing,* he wrote, *and Everything . . . When you knee Terry,*
*Or Joe, or Ed in the balls, you knee me. I tell you, it*

*Matters not who knees you, or whom you knee, only that it*
*Is expected you knee someone, not live in peace, at rest*
*On clouds of joy, like Romans on couches: you need tarry*
*In the fields of love, becoming them . . .* But, lying in wait,
The night flamed before him, buildings crackling. *I am—*
His pen wobbled, nearly shook from his hand—*next—*

—*To myself*. . . It dawned on him. "I've always been next
To myself—" The pen broke from the pressure. He held it
In his palm. "All my life. . . looking sideways at what I am,
Cruel, disgusted—at what I was, would be, all the rest. . ."
What he was now was alarmed. He heard the crashing weight
Of a building collapse, as across the street the old Unitari-

An church flared like a cross. *Smooth as a eunuch, hairy*
*As a coconut, I contain the fires of cities. I am the nex-*
*Us of mirrors, the orange-faced mob, shouting, the weight*
*In caskets at sea, the man who owns an animal, who holds it*
*In his hands at night, the woman who desires solitude, rest.*
*I am him, I am her, I am what I am, and not all that I am . . .*

                       †        †        †

*I am the walrus*, Perry wrote, chuckling. He was getting it.
*Stand and wait* was next; then, *doppelgänger*, and the rest. . .
He hurried to the dictionary to look up the word *unitary*.

## —— 23

Perry pressed the top of his silver pen. *I suffer*
*From all the manias: ego, mono, and megalo,* he wrote.
What he lacked in self-awareness, he told himself,
He made up for in self-laceration. Then the thought
Occurred to him: what did he have in him to praise?
As sometimes happened, at night, his father's voice,

Like a ventriloquist's, threw itself into his voice,
His face taking over his son's: *God, how I suffer!*
Then, softening: *Late in life, you learn to praise*
*The small things. . .* Perry had these lines by rote,
The two flags of that voice signalling his thought
From the deck of a boat drifting between himself—

That useless, rocky precipice—and his other self—
The lighthouse—down the starry river of his voice.
Silent, unsure, staring out the window, Perry thought
He heard Paul's voice, what he'd say now: *Still suffer*
*All the slings & arrows you can, eh, Per?* Perry wrote,
*There is nothing in nature the human voice can praise*

*But the human voice, all other things a song of praise*
*Sung by a different voice.* He felt the years of self-
Pity, years without fury, as he turned a page, wrote:
*Father, when I speak, I speak in someone else's voice.*
*Mother, when I look at women, I see your face, suffer-*
*Ing, mute. I never heard your voice, what you thought—*

"—Of me . . ." It always comes back to me, he thought.
Then, as if pain's voice were itself a kind of praise,
By which a man worships, and escapes worship, to suffer
No longer the bitter, ingenious quarrel against himself,
Perry realized each child learns, modulates, his voice,
Until he sings his song, or songs . . . Quietly, he wrote:

*All songs pre-date their singer, are learned by rote,*
*Until the singer doesn't hear his own words, thoughts;*
*The schizophrenic mind, deaf to itself, its one voice*
*Divorced from meaning, from the world, until its praise*
*Hardens to fury, and furious destruction, finds itself*
*Becoming one with, and praising, a world that suffers . . .*

†     †     †

Perry suffered the night coming on, his every thought
A stone in a cathedral of praise. He heard his voice
Shake itself from itself, begin its song . . . He wrote:

# The Whole Truth

As he walked into the courtroom, Perry Mason
Was looking hard for a needle in a haystack.
Mason's client, the famous Air Force pilot,
To entice Jethro Wyatt's daughter to submit
To his charms, had rented a plane and a long
Banner that read SPREAD 'EM! Unfortunately,

The plane turned upside down. Fortunately—
Though at the prison, his good friend Mason
Had pretended to doubt this, pulling a long
Face—he had landed unhurt in a haystack.
And today, D.A. Hamilton Burger would submit
That the pile of bones and flesh this pilot

Had brutally pulverized was not this pilot
Himself (Burger used the word unfortunately),
But a young woman who had refused to submit
To the kinky desires of a pervert (here Mason
Objected) who wanted a roll in the haystack!
Sustained, for the moment, Mason took a long

Look at the witness, Jethro Wyatt. "How long,
Mr. Wyatt, have the young pilots at the Pilot
Academy been flying low, over that haystack?"
Wyatt cracked his knuckles. "Unfortunately,
I can see what you're driving at, Mr. Mason—
But if you're implying my Misty would submit—"

Mason's voice was ice. "Your Honor, I submit
That resolving this case won't take very long—
If I may digress . . .?" "Proceed, Mr. Mason."
Mason whirled. "Mr. Wyatt, do you own a pilot
License?" Burger leaped up. "Unfortunately,
Mr. Mason, it is the contents of the haystack—"

Mason scowled. "I refer to a second haystack—"
The courtroom erupted—"the evidence I submit
As proof Misty Wyatt is alive. Unfortunately,
Mr. Wyatt, these bones, flesh, and hank of long
Hair dropped from the plane of a second pilot:
Is this pile not Mrs. Wyatt?" thundered Mason.

†       †       †

"Unfortunately, I submit," said Della. "How long
Did we have the wrong haystack?" "The pile: it
Contained her gold ring," grinned Perry Mason.

# Notes

NUMBER 7 quotes verbatim, in the first, second, and sixth stanzas, passages from Michel Foucault's *Histoire de la folie à l'âge classique: Folie et déraison*, as translated by Richard Howard (*Madness and Civilization*, Vintage Books, 1973).

NUMBER 13's first stanza is a paraphrase of material found in Bernard Sichère's article "A partir de Michel Foucalt" (*Tel Quel* 86, Winter, 1980), as quoted by Stephen Bann in "Foucault's Silence" (*PN Review*, no. 26, p. 34).

NUMBER 15 affectionately remembers the Iowa workshop.

NUMBER 18, in particular, uses elements of the minstrel show.

NUMBER 22's first stanza is taken from *Song of Myself*.

This sequence is indebted to the poems of John Berryman and Paul Laurence Dunbar.

Design by David Bullen
Typeset in Mergenthaler Electra
with Deepdene display
Harrington-Young Typesetters
Printed by Haddon Craftsmen
on acid-free paper